FOOTLIGHTS from One Woman's Journey

By Stephanie Chaney Atkins

FOOTLIGHTS from One Woman's Journey

By Stephanie Chaney Atkins

Chaney Redbird Group, LLC.

9301 State Highway 75 South

Unit 653

New Waverly TX 77358-4225

Footlights.OWJ@gmail.com

ISBN: 978-1-7370868-0-2

Acknowledgements

For who makes you different from anyone else? What do you have that you did not receive? And if you did not receive it, why do you boast as though you did not?
I Corinthians 4:7 NIV

No book is written without the support of others; and this one is no exception. It is a mirror and a window into my life. Although we may not have met, you will read our stories. Some of you will know the difference that you have made in my life. Know that I have sought to make good on your investment. And hopefully, all of us will see the horizon of possibilities that beckon us, come.

God gifted me to loving parents, Oscar and Ara Belle, to whom I owe my very existence. I am blessed to have been raised in a family with three brothers, Oscar Charles, Segal, and Sidney, and two sisters, Sylvia and Sabrina. Thank you for the emotional safety and unconditional love of a nurturing family.

I thank God for Brandon, my son, and Brittany, my daughter. For 19 years we were all friends believing that through Christ, we could do all things.

To Dwain, my beloved spouse, thank you for being God's answer to prayers beyond a husband and bringing with you Brian, another son for me to love.

To Shannon (Brandon) and Monique (Brian), our daughters-in-love, you have brought much love to our sons and to our family.

To Gus, Karter, and Landon, our three grandsons, I am grateful to be your NanaLene.

And most of all, I thank Jesus. Nothing is possible without God's amazing grace and mercy.

To Sister Brown

Sunrise: August 27, 1925 – Sunset: August 27, 2018

But if I do not have love, I am nothing. I Corinthians 13:2b NIV

There are no words, only love.

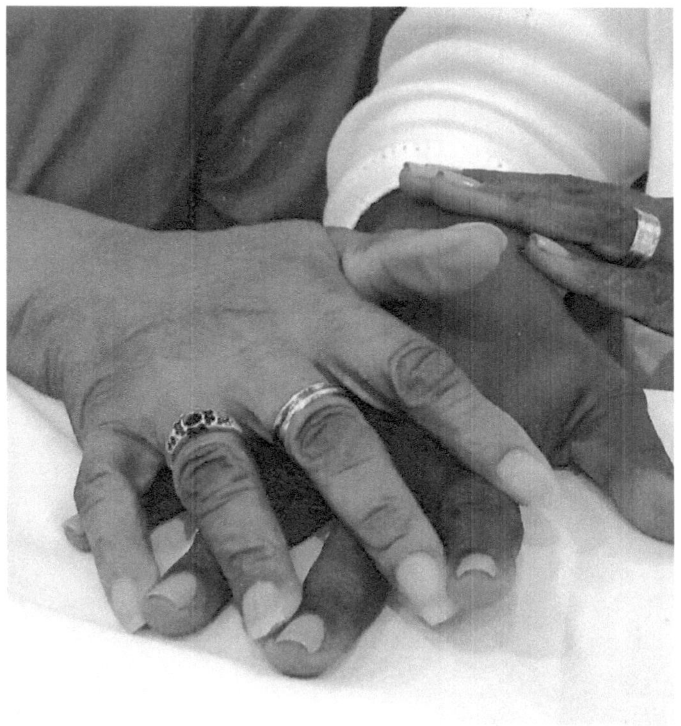

Table of Contents

Her children rise up and call her blessed...many women have done excellently, but you surpass them all. Proverbs 31:28-29

I have the honor of being my mother's first reader. I saw these pages before you (lucky me!). And despite being the one who formed me, the person I've known since before my first breath – I read my mother as a woman for perhaps the first time.

The revelation of Stephanie was a battle of marvels and might. I have always been proud to be my mother's daughter, to declare the statement with ferociousness. I see her when I look in the mirror, in my eyes and wide smile. I feel her when, without notice or reason or rhyme, I have the overwhelming desire to throw my arms out, palms wide and outstretched to the sun, open and full and safe. I've become her when my students and friends repeat her words back to me, and I realize it is because they heard her from me. To them, her words are mine. To me, I am my mother's daughter.

The rare privilege of discovering her within these pages discovered parts of me. My darker moments look different from my mother's though our scars similarly sketch the bark of our skin. My roots she stretched across oceans sprout from seeds shared free in red dirt and the dust that coats our childhoods in a hazy beautiful film that only makes God's patience real and simple and kind. My woman recognized her woman as the starting pieces. It was meeting her again.

So I would like to introduce you to my mother. Here are the things you should know:

- Stephanie Chaney was born in 1959 to Oscar and Ara Belle. She is the product of Georgia clay next to green and yellow and white fields. She is the sum total of tenacity and heart, and prayers from the Souls of Black Folk.
- My mother is so vibrant that her colors appear surely as a sign that God's light reflects by design.
- My mother is weather. Not a singular element or season; she is the storm and the sun, the winter clouds and spring rains and waves. She is air and rumble and the force that shakes the very ground.
- My mother's nickname is etched into my skin. Her words have formed our lives.
- My mother is a wonder.

In these pages, Stephanie is brave and open, revealing parts of herself she never thought possible. She unlocks some earned truths yet just scratches the surface of her beautiful, tragically triumphant complexity and worth. My mother's life appears between these pages, and yet it shows only the glimpses of her majesty. She has many stories, but she finds her truth and faith in these. They are our favorites.

Proverbs 31:31 emboldens, *"Honor her for all that her hands have done, and let her works bring praise at the city gate."* For all that she's made, I am grateful and formed, and for this that her hands have made, I am extraordinarily proud.
I hope her journey inspires and encourages you. May God's purpose in your life manifest through faith that stirs right here and right now.

And may you love Stephanie as we do, wholeheartedly and in awe.

Here's to you, Stellaluna – look what you did!

This is the book I've been writing for a long time. My first journals date back to high school. My writings have mostly been letters to God, reflections on my journey, a winding path with peaks and valleys. Years ago, a good friend told me that since God knows everything, I didn't need to write to Him! Yet, the more I have reflected, the more journals I have filled.

This book is a collection of my stories that I share in hopes that someone else traveling a winding path with their own peaks and valleys may be encouraged. Who cares? Good question. Maybe no one. Maybe you. And, if it is you, then it is for you that I have chosen to push past the critic that shows up in all of us when we step out into unchartered waters, when we don't know what will happen. I am reminded that all of us live in the shadow of God's amazing mercy and grace and His Blood covers all of our steps.

Above all, in writing these stories, I have sought to be honest with myself.

> *I have to live with myself and so,*
> *I want to be fit for myself to know.*
> *I want to be able as days go by,*
> *Always to look myself straight in the eye.*

These are the opening lines from Edgar Guest's poem "Myself", which our mom regularly recited to me and my siblings growing up, subtly instilling lessons about character and integrity. The poem continues to be a plumb line for me. I have included it in its entirety at the end of the book.

At the end of each story, you will find:

 my learnings

 verses from God's Word, The Holy Bible
I have used the King James Version (KJV) and the New International Version (NIV);
noted as such after each Scripture.

 a few prompts to encourage you to capture your thoughts and
feelings about what you have learned and are learning on your journey; perhaps
starting a journal or simply adding to one you may already keep.

My Footlights

Footlights have been described as a row of lights across the front of a stage floor.
My Footlights are lessons learned across the stage floor of my life. Serendipitously, I
think that you will discover some shared adventures, albeit we are strangers! I
invite you to sojourn with me.

His Lamp and Lights

Thy Word is a lamp for my feet and a light on my path. Psalm 119:105 NIV

*For I know the plans I have for you, declares the Lord, plans to prosper you and not
to harm you, plans to give you hope and a future.* Jeremiah 29:11 NIV

*Ah, Sovereign Lord, You have made the heavens and the earth by Your great power
and outstretched arm. Nothing is too hard for You.* Jeremiah 32:17 NIV

Your Footlights

What's stirring within you as we begin our journey together?

The Story of the Red Bird

I grew up in rural middle Georgia where there wasn't a single traffic light in our small town. And forget streetlights because there were no streets out in the country, only dirt roads that looked like worn weathered leather stripes separating cotton and peanut fields. We finally got paved roads when I was in middle school.

We lived on the same dirt road as Granny Lou, my dad's mother, and two of my dad's brothers. There were three houses about a half mile from each other; our house was in the middle. That was a good thing since we loved to hang out with Granny Lou. No matter when we showed up, Granny Lou took the time to see us. She stopped whatever she was doing and gave us her full attention along with some kind of yummy treat like the good ice cream in the round carton (at our house, ice cream was in a box) or homemade tea cakes.

Even more than we loved those special treats, we loved listening to Granny Lou's stories about when she was a little girl. Like the one about puppies...she and her five siblings would make puppies and hide them under the bed. What kind of people make puppies? And then hide them under a bed? Hmmm? These puppies were fruit turnovers, sometimes filled with sweet Georgia peaches, or plump juicy blackberries; Granny Lou and her siblings hid them to surprise their dad when he came home from a day of working in the fields.

Another story was about what she had learned from her mother about the power of gentle communication. When she misbehaved, she remembered her mother's scolding as more of a whisper. There was no need for ranting - gentleness prevailed. She must have known about Proverbs 15:1a ...*'a gentle answer turns away wrath'*.

My all-time favorite story was about the red bird. Growing up in Georgia, we would often see red birds. Their magnificent color made them easy to spot. Granny Lou told us to blow a kiss to the red bird because it was a message from God: God was watching out for us and something special was about to happen.

Granny Lou has long been gone. And I now know that red birds are cardinals, and that God is always watching out for us. I have also come to know that 'red birds' are not always birds.

Like when a high school teacher offered me more than a summer job:

> I was all set to go off to college, or so I thought, until I learned that the total costs for my first year exceeded what I had accumulated between scholarships, money from my mom and dad, and my savings from my job as a waitress at the local Days Inn Tasty World Restaurant. Unfortunately, there were not many options for summer jobs in our small town. The restaurant had closed, and the other local businesses were primarily gas stations. And then one Wednesday night at church youth group, a friend told me about his summer job working for one of our high school teachers. She had secured a contract with the U.S. Census and was looking for workers to complete the U.S. Census for elderly people in surrounding rural counties who were not able to complete it for themselves. I reached out to our teacher; she hired me; and so began a summer of daily conversations with residence historians. While I completed census forms, I listened to their life stories which had a conspicuous consistent theme: through it all, the Lord had made a way! Many years later, I have my own testimony about God's way-making and that high school teacher is ever dear to me. Red birds!

Like when I moved to Houston, Texas:

> I was a thirty-year-old single mom living in Cleveland, Ohio with a seven-year-old son and a three-year-old daughter, when I mustered enough faith to apply for a higher-level job with the same company in Houston, Texas, where I knew absolutely no one. And exercising more faith, I flew to

Houston, Texas for the interview. My faith was rewarded -- I was offered the job immediately! *"What now? Where would we live? What about school for my children? What about childcare?"* The questions would not stop! And the hiring manager wanted my answer. I needed help. I reached out to our pastor and explained my dilemma: stay in Cleveland, Ohio in the same job with support from my aunt and uncle *or* move to Houston, Texas for a job promotion with no family or any other kind of support system. Pastor listened, attested God's Sovereignty, and closed our meeting with a prayer re-iterating that the same God that I trusted in Cleveland, Ohio was also in Houston, Texas. Would I trust and believe? I accepted the job. A red bird wrapped in an encouraging word!

Within a couple of weeks I flew to Houston again, this time to find a house. By midday on the second day, I had found our dream house...three bedrooms, two and a half baths, back porch swing, fenced-in backyard; in a top-rated school system. And when the real estate agent and I walked into the backyard, there perched on the fence, was a red bird, seemingly just waiting for us to show up...and we did not disappoint!

And finally, like when I had run out of energy moving to Anchorage, Alaska:
> Now in my late thirties, my son was thirteen, and my daughter was nine when we relocated from Houston, Texas to Anchorage, Alaska. The weeks leading up to the move had been exhausting. Everywhere I looked, there was more stuff to sort through. Where had all this stuff come from?

> The frenetic busyness of packing finally ended when the moving truck pulled away. I was now on my way to say good-bye to a dear friend. I walked in the back door like all good friends. She welcomed me with an embrace that spelled L-O-V-E in every language! I made my way to my favorite chair: a large, overstuffed round chair, made just for curling up; I plopped down. One long inhale followed by one long exhale and I was purring; more truthfully snoring and drooling! Not sure how long I had been asleep before I awakened to my friend serving me a cup of hot tea.

What a special treat, especially for a single mom! With that cup of tea, my friend hydrated my body and refreshed my soul...my red bird!

Yes, sometimes a 'red bird' can be an encouraging word, a person like my high school teacher, a cup of tea...maybe even a smile, a handwritten note, a text message, or a call. An open heart is all that it takes to see a red bird. Be sure to keep the eyes of your heart open!

My Footlights

God is ever present in our lives. He never leaves us; He never forsakes us. Yet in the ups and downs of everyday living, we forget. Friends have shared their red bird stories, such as feathers appearing out of nowhere, or the sun suddenly peering from behind the clouds, or a double rainbow, or the presence of any type of bird. I have also heard stories about cardinals being visitors from heaven. I believe that all of these may be true, but I am sticking with Granny Lou. My heart still skips a beat whenever I see a red bird, I blow a kiss, gently whisper a prayer of hope and watch for something special. Odd thing is that when I watch for something special, I find it!

A few fun facts about cardinals from "World Birds". (www.worldbirds.org)
1. The cardinal is a symbol of confidence and balance; portrayed mainly as a reassuring sign.
2. Cardinals mate for life.
3. Cardinals are named as a state bird for seven states: Illinois, Indiana, Ohio, Kentucky, North Carolina, West Virginia, and Virginia.

His Lamp and Lights

The Lord Himself goes before you and will be with you; He will never leave you nor forsake you. Do not be afraid; do not be discouraged. Deuteronomy 31:8 NIV

And we know that in all things God works for the good of those who love him, who have been called according to His purpose. Romans 8:28 NIV

Before they call, I will answer; while they are still speaking, I will hear. Isaiah 65:24 NIV

What's your red bird? How do you feel when you see it?

Filling Tanks

Donned in borrowed snow boots and my Georgia winter coat with a weekly bus pass, I was ready to begin my job hunt by plastering resumes across downtown Cleveland, Ohio. Not so easy, I learned. *'No Applications Accepted'* signs seemed to be posted everywhere; of the seven businesses I approached in the first couple of hours, only two would even take my resume. I felt like a country bumpkin – small town girl in a big city thinking that I could just find a job by putting in unsolicited applications! What was I thinking?

Only a few days earlier I had been in Georgia planning to get married in December and begin our new life in Pensacola, Florida. Those plans had come to a screeching halt when a woman making the exact same plans as me (literally to marry the same guy) called to let me know! Now what?

Nothing short of divine intervention revealed Plan B. My dear aunt, Sister Brown, just happened to be in Georgia visiting when I got that phone call. She had recently become an empty nester and invited me to live with her. After an eighteen-hour car ride, I was living in Cleveland, Ohio and making plans to find a job.

It was too early to go back home. Where else could I go? I looked up and down the streets for recognizable company names when I spotted Kelly Services, a staffing company best known for Kelly Girls, primarily placing women in temporary office clerical assignments. I walked in the door; the receptionist's call seemed to go on for a while, but I did not mind as I enjoyed a brief respite from The Hawk, the notorious Cleveland wind whipping across Lake Erie.

"How can I help you?" I told her I was looking for a job and hoping that Kelly Services might have some kind of management training program. No; however, they were always looking for clerical help, expert typists. When I told her that I didn't have a typing score, she looked confused, like *why are you even here*? I could feel the water trying to find a release in my eyes. I dared not blink. After what felt like a whole five minutes, she smiled and encouraged me to complete an application in the chance (albeit slim to none) they received an assignment that didn't require a typing score. I completed the application and walked outside to be instantly reacquainted with the Hawk!

For the next few weeks despite increasing doubts, I persistently faced the piercing Hawk with an equally strong determination believing that I could find a job. No leads, not even a conversation beyond that awkward exchange with the Kelly Services receptionist. What if I couldn't find a job? I knew that I could always go home. My parents had encouraged me to move to Cleveland to pursue my dreams but made sure that I knew that they would always welcome me home with open arms! But returning home to a small town with few job options had no appeal. I had graduated from college. I was ready to begin my career. I wanted more!

And then one day the call came: Kelly Services had an assignment at the Western Advertising Company, no typing required! I was so excited. I wondered what I would be doing at an advertising company. Maybe I would be writing ads, I had taken a couple of college classes. Maybe this assignment would lead to a full-time job – just like in my imagination! The instructions were simple: arrive at 8 A.M., wear comfortable shoes, and ask for Irene. I could do this.

I arrived at 7:15 A.M. to a warehouse. An advertising office in a warehouse? Knowing that I am directionally challenged, I double-checked the address. I was at the correct address. Oh well, you can't judge a book by the cover. Wearing my best navy-blue skirt, starched white blouse, and a pair of stylish flats, I confidently pushed the door open. The concrete floor was bare except for a steel desk in the middle and a security attendant. I asked for Irene and within minutes, a fifty-ish or so woman appeared.

Irene was also dressed in a skirt and blouse though she sported black oxford support shoes, maybe the kind with steel toe protection. I dutifully followed her down a long, equally bare cold corridor to a room with rows of tables neatly stacked with colorful paper that looked like the inserts for a Sunday newspaper. Interesting. Irene explained that I would be assembling advertising flyers for various clients. Could this be the assignment? For sure, I didn't need a typing score. Did I finish college to assemble advertising flyers? Disappointment surged from my feet to my head.

Irene's glance caught my wet eyes. She paused for a moment, smiled kindly, and asked if I was ready to begin the assignment. I wanted to run away screaming how unfair this felt. Instead, I cleared my throat; hoping in some way that that would also clear my mind. With a deep breath, I uttered "Yes, I would give it a go.". Something had to be better than nothing! I began to assemble the flyers. When I did look up at the ticking clock on the bare concrete wall, it was 5 P.M.; time to go home.

I made my way to the bus station against the Hawk. There were a lot more people catching the bus at rush hour. I was relieved to get a seat after I had been standing all day. I got off at my regular stop and walked home, where Sister Brown was ready to hear about my day, my new job. Her warm touch released the opening of a dam that I had forced shut for way too long. I could not stop the flood of tears. I had so many pent-up hurts...my shattered dreams of getting married, my doubting the decision to leave Georgia, my naivete about how to find a job, my shame about stuffing advertising flyers with a college degree. How could God give me this assignment? I had prayed every morning and every night and believed that God would answer my prayers.

Sister Brown turned the pages of her weathered Bible to Colossians 3:23: *Whatever you do, do to the glory of God*. She continued to read it aloud until I finally looked up. Our eyes met again and without uttering a word, I knew that this was my mandate. That evening, I made my way to bed earlier than usual pondering how I could stuff flyers to God's glory??

Though forlorn by the mundaneness of days becoming weeks and weeks turning into months, I went to work every day, arriving early, smartly dressed in those black oxford support shoes (no steel-toes) and performed my work as though I were working for God, which did not go unnoticed by Irene. After nearly three months, Irene called me into the office. I was curious, though not concerned, as Irene and I had developed a friendship, often sharing life stories at lunch time. She had good news. She had recommended me for a new Kelly Services assignment that required a person who was timely, trustworthy, and reliable. *That Kelly Services receptionist had remembered me and called Irene for feedback.* I thanked Irene. I did not get a seat on the bus ride home that day and it did not matter. I was excited, looking forward to a new assignment! The next morning could not come fast enough.

I reported to Kelly Services to learn about my assignment. I thanked the receptionist for remembering me. She smiled as she described that my assignment would be located in downtown Cleveland in a newly designed office suite for an oil and gas company. No more warehouse! An office building! An oil and gas company! Quite encouraging...until. Until she shared that a food company that had been awarded a contract for their recently patented coffee machines needed someone to operate them. *What?* From stuffing advertising flyers to filling coffee pots??

As I pondered my decision, I caught the eyes of the receptionist. She was still smiling; I imagined her feeling pretty good about what she had done...she'd remembered me for what seemed to be an assignment with potential. I said "yes", choosing to rise above the familiar pit of disappointment and the humbling reality of no other employment options. The training session would begin as soon as I could get to the building, which was a couple of blocks away; an easy trek now that there was no Hawk! It was April.

Jim, a forty-ish year old salesman, expressed his excitement about landing the contract for his company and then having the ingenious idea to have a Kelly Girl operate the coffee machines. He explained that operating the machines was fairly straightforward: empty the pre-measured pack of coffee into the filter and press the start button. There were 12 coffee stations scattered throughout two floors that were to be filled by 6:00 A.M., constantly refilled until noon, and then thoroughly cleaned. Oh, and my work schedule would be from 5:30 A.M. to 1:30 P.M., Monday through Friday, and I would begin the job on the following Monday. I set out for the bus, got a seat, and made my way home pondering making coffee to God's glory.

When I got home, Sister Brown was waiting for me. She had been wondering about an unusual dream she had the night before about me filling tanks at a gas station. We were both curious and left it at that. I went on to share the details of my new assignment expressing my disappointment. Unbeknownst to me, she was contemplating the correlation of filling coffee pots at an oil and gas company to filling gas tanks at a gas station. She concluded that her dream was God's confirmation of my new assignment, a divine placement. Gas tanks, coffee pots – no difference to me – clearly not my dream job!

With my new habit of doing my best as if working for God, I started my new assignment filling coffee tanks. At least this time, I was in an office environment and imagined that just maybe - somehow, someway, this assignment might lead to a full-time job. Whenever I made coffee for a meeting, I made sure the coffee space was spotless! Before long, I became known as the coffee girl looking for a job. Six months into the assignment, the receptionist position at the office suite became vacant. And while my aspirations were grander, the receptionist job could be that notional foot in the door. Besides, I would be receiving benefits, something that I had never had. I was hired. And so, the coffee girl became the receptionist!

From the receptionist role came jobs of increasing responsibility in Human Resources for thirty years; and then for the last five years, a venture into the world of Ethics and Compliance, beginning in Cleveland, Ohio to Houston, Texas to Anchorage, Alaska to London, England to Baltimore, Maryland and back to Houston, Texas.

Imagine the testimony thirty-five years later, when the coffee girl who became the receptionist retired as a Vice President from that same oil and gas company following an international career! A divine placement, indeed.

A lot of life also happens during a 35 year career…getting married; having a son and a daughter; getting divorced; flying solo as a parent for 19 years; being brave enough to move around the world with that son and daughter giving them perspective beyond their backyard and watching them demonstrate the discipline it takes to march across university commencement stages and emerge as responsible world citizens; long-time friends introducing me to their friend who had also been flying solo for twenty years raising his son; marrying him seven months later with the blessing of another son, and … I pause. Neither time nor space offer expressions to capture all the mountains, valleys, and in-betweens. And, I don't even begin to know how to express my overflow of thanks to my family who have again and again tirelessly demonstrated their unconditional loving support. And even if I were an octopus, there still would not be enough arms to wrap around the friends, whether for a season or ever yet enduring, who have blessed my life.

What I can do is render thanks to a Sovereign God for all that He has done and is doing in me!

My Footlights

Be brave and explore opportunities. Turn over every rock. Dream big. Persevere. And finally, keep filling the tanks wherever you are to the glory of God!

His Light and Lamp

Whatever you do, work at it with all your heart, as working for the Lord, not human masters. Colossians 3:23 NIV

Now unto Him who is able to do exceedingly abundantly above all that we can ask or think, according to the Power that worketh in us. Ephesians 3:20 KJV

Being confident of this, He who began a good work in you will carry it on to completion until the day of Christ Jesus. Philippians 1:6 NIV

Your Footlights

What tanks are you filling? Are you about ready to give up? What keeps you going?

And Now I See

After I had been working for about six months as a receptionist, I was ready to move into my first apartment. I did not know the city well enough to know the best places to look; I did not have a lot of money, nor did I have a car; but what I did have was a new friend from work who recommended the apartment complex where she lived. The property had one room efficiency units and as a bonus, she offered that I could commute to work with her. I applied and was approved! And just like that, God answered both of my prayers: a new home and a way to get to work.

That one room efficiency on the second floor was enough until I got pregnant and got married. In that one room, I had a single bed, a second-hand dresser, a TV tray, a TV, and one chair. After we were married, we moved into a two-family house, closer to my husband's family. One family lived on the first floor and our family lived on the second floor.

> *Our marriage was struggling to survive my husband's parade of extra marital affairs. I kept hoping that being a good wife would be enough; that somehow the infidelity would finally come to an end and that all would be well for our young family. My hopes cratered when I learned that one of his girlfriends was pregnant just as I was, this time with our second child. That bolstered me to face the hard, cold truth that the marriage was over. With a baby girl in my tummy and a little boy squeezing my hand, I stepped out on faith to make a new life for me, for us. We never looked back.*

Now a family of three, we -- me, a four-year old son, and a newborn daughter -- moved back to that same, first apartment complex, this time in a two-bedroom apartment on the third floor. And thanks to my parents, we had a car - a used, two-door green Ford Granada. In yet another expression of unconditional love, my parents made the eighteen-hour drive from Georgia, 1000 plus miles, to bring that car to us. Once again, God provided!

Our comings and goings looked a bit like a mini caravan traversing three flights of stairs at least twice a day. A young professional woman carrying a baby girl, a diaper bag, and a briefcase - followed closely by a four-year old little boy clutching his backpack that held his treasured possessions like Ninja Turtles and Cherry Fruit Roll-Ups. Up and down and up and down. We left in the dark and came home in the dark.

Inside our apartment, we were safe from the sounds and smells that lurked all around us. Outside our apartment, there was non-stop arguing, constant activity, and musty smells from the worn carpet and marijuana (illegal then and now). Despite what was going on around us, no one ever bothered us; not even a knock on our door. Whenever my family from Georgia visited, my mom expressed concern about our well-being. She worried about us; she asked if I was afraid. No, we were at home. I had come to know that the same God who protected me growing up in a home on a dirt road in rural Georgia also protected us in an apartment in urban Cleveland, Ohio.

Still, I wanted better. I dreamed of buying a house with a backyard for my children to run and play. But unless I did some things differently, it would remain only a dream. I needed to save money for a down payment. That meant paying off credit card debts that had amassed when there was more month than money. I needed help; so I went to Consumer Credit Counseling Services. I cut up the credit cards even though I could not imagine that we could make it from paycheck to paycheck without them. The credit counselor put together a debt repayment plan and a sustainable budget including the occasional shared McDonald's hotcakes and sausage on Saturday mornings. I also joined the company savings plan through payroll deductions where my contributions would be matched by the company - one of those benefits that I never had until now.

It took two years (that was two *long* one-year leases), to pay off my debts and save enough to buy our first home. God sent a savvy real estate agent Sheila K., who just happened to be a former single mother, to help us find our new home, a house with that backyard for my children to run and play. Within weeks, we found a house, and moving day could not come fast enough. However, there was one outstanding piece of business, I had to complete a final cleaning of our apartment.

About an hour after the moving truck finished unloading our household goods, I got in my trusty green Ford Granada and began the familiar drive back to our apartment building. Somehow, this time felt different.

> *I entered the property site littered with all kinds of stuff and parked in front of a dilapidated building. The people standing in front seemed menacing. I walked into a grimy foyer. I forcibly inhaled the musty scent of lingering marijuana. I climbed three long flights of stairs. I approached a weathered brown door, turned my key, and walked inside.*

I stood quietly beholding what had been and what would be no more. As I began to clean our apartment for the last time came my Damascus Road (Acts 9) moment when God removed His protective screen from my eyes to see what others had seen: an apartment complex infested with drugs, their dealers, and too many others who seemingly had given up on their hopes and dreams for anything better. And how He had kept us safe from hurt, harm, and danger! Decades later, the complex has long been demolished; yet, God is still keeping us as only He can. Amen!

A Note:
Consumer Credit Counseling Services
Consumer Credit Counseling Services help overextended credit users eliminate high interest rate credit and debt. It is their mission to help you regain financial stability. Certified credit counselors evaluate your debts, budget, and credit. Then they help you identify the best way to get out of debt in your situation. October 6, 2020, World Wide Web.

My Footlights

I give thanks to God for His unconditional love, protection, and provision. Only until He prepared another place for me and my two little children, did He graciously open my eyes to show me where we had been and how He had kept us safely in the palm of his Hand! Although trying and tedious, I am also grateful for the diligence to pay off my debts and the discipline to save money; building on life lessons from my dad who says that you cannot borrow your way of out of debt (though so tempted by offers for debt consolidation loans) and from my mom who ever reminded us that money spends one time (once it's spent, it's gone). I know what faith in God can do.

His Lamp and Light

And Elisha prayed, "Open his eyes, Lord, so that he may see". Then the Lord opened the servant's eyes, and he looked and saw the hills full of horses and chariots of fire all around. Elisha. 2 Kings 6:17 NIV

No eye has seen, no ear has heard, no mind has conceived what God has prepared for those who love Him. 1 Corinthians 2:9 NIV

For His anger lasts only a moment, but His favor lasts a lifetime; weeping may stay for the night; but rejoicing comes in the morning. Psalm 30:5 NIV

YOUR FOOTLIGHTS

When have your eyes been opened so that you could see differently? How are you seeing with the eyes of your heart? Are you being the best steward of what God has given to you?

Climbing The Mountain

How did I get here? I was in my early 40's and had traveled to Aberdeen, Scotland from Houston, Texas. Here was a village farmhouse in a valley surrounded by mountains that were still green though the chill in the air let you know that those tops would soon be capped with snow. I sat with a cup of hot tea nestled in a comfy chair in a circle of strangers who had also found their own comfy chair. We were gathered for a one-week residential course on personal coaching. Our leaders, one male and one female, described the cadence for the week as three sessions per day, shared meals, interspersed with regular walks to enjoy our beautiful surroundings. And the crowning point of the week was to be a mountain climb.

Wait, what was that last part? Did she say a mountain climb? My thoughts were hijacked! I could hear chatter in the background...one lady with curly hair talked about the highs that she'd experienced on mountain climbs around the world, most recently in Peru. Another guy had climbed Kilimanjaro. Another lady shared that climbing was one of her family's favorite outings. Every story sounded like a stone rolling downhill until the chatter boomed like an avalanche! I scanned the room and quickly concluded that I was the most non-athletic one in the group. That nagging extra 20 pounds now felt like 50+ pounds. I didn't have time to exercise! *Yes, I would most certainly embarrass myself.* In a nano second, I had become obsessed with the mountain climb.

It was time to begin our first session. I repositioned myself in an effort to refocus my attention away from the cloud that had formed over my head. It only kind of worked. I made it through Day 1. My cloud faithfully followed me into dinner and then to bed making good on a fitful night of sleep. Now it was Day 2, and we strangers were quickly becoming friends as we were coaching each other through our life stories. Sometimes, I became so enthralled in the conversations that I forgot about my cloud.

On Day 3, I was feeling tired from a lack of sleep. Despite trying my best, my cloud was not going away. Our afternoon session was about dismantling made-up stories that get in the way of our own success. Our leaders asked for volunteers to share experiences and insights with these made-up stories. I was now amongst friends (*strange that spending time together, regardless of who or where one is, is often an inroad to friendship*) which made it easier to unveil the dark cloud of fears that I had made up about the mountain climb. My new friends unanimously allayed my concerns with assurances of support. One of the leaders even offered to stay back with me to demonstrate that there was no pressure to join the climb. The choice would be mine. That was unbelievably generous given the collective zest for the outdoors!

Their assurances, like rays of sunshine, slowly pierced through my cloud. Emotionally drained from unveiling my fears, I made my way to my room. I snuggled into bed for some much-needed sleep, only to experience my own wrestling match. In Corner 1 was FACT, assurances from the entire class, and in Corner 2 was FICTION, the made-up stories in my mind. Morning dawned with little rest: the emerging winner was FICTION: the made-up stories! Exasperating!

By the start of class on Day 4, I decided to declare that I would not join the climb. My friends reluctantly accepted my decision and "poof!" went my cloud as we wrapped up the week's learnings. After dinner, I climbed into bed and fell asleep before I could even reflect on my decision. I awakened refreshed.

Day 5! The mountain climb was to begin after breakfast. I had opted to go into the village for the day. The energy in the room was high, lots of laughter! And I was looking forward to discovering the quaintness of the small village. We began the day as usual with a check-in. There was another person in our circle. He was introduced as Mike, a climb master with extensive experience on this particular mountain. He had a quiet demeanor and a warm smile. Mike reviewed the safety protocols for the climb and asked the group to gather in teams of four persons.

The groups were forming, and I was gathering my things to head off to the meeting point when Mike asked to speak to me privately.

He wanted to know more about my decision to not join the climb. I shared my concern about not being in good enough physical shape to make the climb; hence risking embarrassment and more importantly, I did not want to take away from the group experience. He listened generously and further described his years of experience which made him confident that I could make the climb. *How could he know? He had just met me!* I tried to convince him that I was different, the exception to all his experiences! And then he made me an offer: simply step in his foot tracks and to let him know when I became tired. When I became tired, we would stop, take a rest, and continue. I was intrigued by such a simple offer. As though he could read my next objection, he went on to assure me that his offer would not impede his commitment to the group for a great climb. Finally, he asked me to simply trust him. I said yes. I cancelled my trip to the village and joined the group. They were all surprised and began to cheer me on.

Mike and I would be a team of two. He pointed out the markers that would keep all of us on the same trail. And the climb began. Mike took a step and I stepped in his tracks. He took another step and I stepped in his tracks. Mike's attempts at conversation were short-circuited by my one-word responses as I singularly focused my eyes on his tracks. We continued until he asked if I needed a break. I said yes. We sat on a rock; I rested. I could see the other climbers frolicking up the mountain. After a brief rest, Mike took a step and I stepped in his tracks. We reached the halfway point and the group gathered for a check-in. Mike completed the group check, and we were off for the second half of the climb. All seemed well. Mike and I continued our cadence; he took a step, and I took a step in his tracks. We were in a groove; and then we stopped. I was curious since I had not asked for a break. He asked me to look up. We had reached the top and the view was breathtaking! I gasped, exhaled slowly to release those made-up stories that had threatened to rob me of this euphoric moment and inhaled even slower to savor a sweetness that only comes from moving beyond stories to simply trusting.

My Footlights

Mike joined the class for our final session to talk about lessons learned from the climb. The group said that Mike's confidence in them gave them the opportunity for a fun climb…they were not competing; they were not pressured to demonstrate prowess; they could focus on the experience. I had learned the power of following a trusted guide step by step only to lift my eyes to an amazing mountaintop view, without a cloud in sight! We too have a Trusted Guide, who invites us to follow Him step by step. Such breathtaking adventures await us…oh, to simply trust and believe!

His Lamps and Lights

I lift up my eyes to the mountains, where does my help come from? My help comes from the Lord, the Maker of heaven and earth. He will not let your foot slip – He who watches over you will not slumber. Psalm 121:1-3 NIV

I can do all this through Christ who gives me strength. Philippians 4:13 NIV

Yet he (Abraham) did not waiver through unbelief regarding the promise of God but was strengthened in his faith and gave glory to God, being fully persuaded that God had power to do what He had promised. Romans 4:20, 21 NIV

YOUR FOOTLIGHTS

What's your mindset when it comes to trying something new? Can you describe a time when you gave up before you tried? What did you learn?

Keep Walking Lene

My mom is not quite sure when I began to walk; however, what she does remember is that I was flat-footed. Today, thanks to my mom, I have arches in both feet after wearing Buster Brown orthopedic high-topped white leather shoes for five years. And thanks to Granny Lou, I am known affectionately as Lene, in honor of Delena, a town somewhere along her travels.

I had been with the company for about thirty years in various Human Resources roles. I had a proven track record of leading teams and knowing how to get things done at all levels in the organization. I wanted to broaden my experience to Ethics and Compliance, which seemed to be a great complement to what I had done already. I expressed interest when I learned of an open position. I was invited to go through a selection process along with experienced external applicants. This was different as most executive positions were internal placements.

At the same time, I reached out to Sister Brown for intercessory prayer, the very same Sister Brown who had declared my coffee girl days as a divine placement. The selection process seemed to be moving toward a favorable outcome; and then, things stalled. I became increasingly weary after a few weeks and called Sister Brown for a word of encouragement. Her advice was simple: "Keep walking Lene and when you get there, the door will be opened, even without your pushing it".

I soon learned that the choice had been narrowed to two candidates: me and an external candidate who had a rather extensive background of skills and experiences in Ethics and Compliance. I closed my last interview with a gardening analogy that I hoped would tip the scales in my favor...while the external candidate undoubtedly had the fertilizer, I knew how and where to use the fertilizer. I did not get the job; the hiring manager chose the candidate with deep expertise.

Though nursing my disappointment, I reached out to the hiring manager to offer assistance to the successful candidate. After all, I did know how and where to use the fertilizer. The hiring manager accepted my offer. She also let me know that I had made the choice difficult and that she would definitely keep me in mind for other openings. And so, I kept walking.

Imagine my great surprise when a month later the hiring manager offered me the position. Turns out that the more experienced candidate decided to pursue another role. *Hmmm…*I kept walking and when I got there, the door was opened!

My Footlights

Walking and waiting are often traveling companions. While you're walking, God is working! Growth can happen at all ages and stages. Finding open doors often requires courage, faith, and perseverance. It is so tempting to give in to what looks like disappointment. I did not get the job initially; but I did get the chance to prove my commitment to the company. Be bold; do not give up!

For the past year, I have been walking a few miles every day. My mantra: Keep walking, Lene. When I say it, even dare to repeat it, I am energized to keep walking! I am curious about what doors might be opening.

His Lamps and Lights

The king's heart is in the hand of the Lord; He directs it like a watercourse wherever He pleases. Proverbs 21:1 NIV

Now faith is the substance of things hoped for and the evidence of things not seen. Hebrews 11: 1 KJV

And without faith it is impossible to please God, because anyone who comes to Him must believe that He exists and that He rewards those who earnestly seek Him. Hebrews 11:6 NIV

YOUR FOOTLIGHTS

I am curious about what's opening for you. Where's your favorite place to walk? What door might be opened if you keep walking?

In the deafening silence, I heard God say to look to Him for great things.

Cleveland, Ohio had been in our rearview mirror for about two years. We were now moving through life in Katy, Texas with the Boy Scouts, Daisy Girl Scouts, Wednesday night suppers at church with Bible Studies, soccer games on Saturdays, after church lunch at Luby's on Sundays. And, on one ordinary day an old friend from Cleveland called to let me know that my former husband was getting married. I was not surprised. We rarely heard from him since we had moved to Texas and after all his shenanigans, I imagined that there must have been a line-up of hopefuls.

*Despite my head's knowledge that I had made the best decision to move forward without him in our lives, everywhere inside salt was finding its way into wounds that I thought had healed. It just did not seem fair. I had not even had a date! One evening, after an especially long day, I knelt next to my bed lamenting to God about the unfairness of it all. The tears subsided out of sheer exhaustion; that is when I believe I heard God promise things beyond good - **<u>GREAT</u>.** I climbed into bed and pondered what I had heard. Sleep found me. I awakened with a restored soul. I reached for my daily devotional; that day's reading was Psalm 91. Verses 15 and 16 were divine red birds.*

This book is a realization of great things He promised, the substance of long-lived hopes, dreams, and good intentions. I am in the fall season of life experiencing hallmarks such as raising a family as a single parent of one son and one daughter, and retiring from one company after 35 years. Many chapters have come to a close, while other chapters are still yet opening.

I will keep walking. I will keep asking for courage, faith, and perseverance. And I will keep believing that when I get there, the door will be opened! With cautious optimism, I look forward to more Footlights. With faith in God, I look forward to more than I could ever think, ask, or imagine!

His Best Is My Prayer For YOU! And I believe that the best is yet to come!

My Footlights

O God of new beginnings and second chances, here I come AGAIN. Thank You God for AGAIN.

His Lamp and Lights

Forget the former things; do not dwell on the past. See, I am doing a new thing! Now it springs up; do you not perceive it? I am making a way in the desert and streams in the wasteland. Isaiah 43:18-19 NIV

But seek ye first the kingdom of God, and His righteous; and all these things shall be added unto you. Matthew 6:33 KJV

If God is for us, who can be against us? Romans 8:31b NIV

The Lord your God is with you, He is mighty to save. He will take great delight in you, He will quiet you with His love, He will rejoice over you with singing. Zephaniah 3:17 NIV

Your Footlights

What is God calling you to trust Him for?

Epigraph

"Myself" by Edgar Guest

I have to live with myself and so
I want to be fit for myself to know.
I want to be able as days go by,
always to look myself straight in the eye;
I don't want to stand with the setting sun
and hate myself for the things I have done.
I don't want to keep on a closet shelf
a lot of secrets about myself
and fool myself as I come and go
into thinking no one else will ever know
the kind of person I really am,
I don't want to dress up myself in sham.
I want to go out with my head erect
I want to deserve all men's respect;
but here in the struggle for fame and wealth
I want to be able to like myself.
I don't want to look at myself and know
I am bluster and bluff and empty show.
I never can hide myself from me;
I see what others may never see;
I know what others may never know,
I never can fool myself and so,
whatever happens I want to be
self respecting and conscience free.

FOOTLIGHTS from One Woman's Journey

By Stephanie Chaney Atkins

The END